**4** Sunita collected the following data during a survey of pupils in her class.

| | Favourite outings | | |
|---|---|---|---|
| | Ice Rink | Cinema | Swimming Pool |
| **Girls** | 3 | 4 | ? |
| **Boys** | 7 | 2 | 11 |

39 pupils took part in the survey.

**How many girls said the swimming pool was their favourite outing?**

**A** 10          **B** 28          **C** 2          **D** 12          **E** 32

**5** Carmel draws a plan of her school using a scale of 1 cm to 5 m.
On the plan, the playground is 6 cm long.

**What is the real length of the playground?**

**A** 6 m          **B** 30 m          **C** 11 m          **D** 7 m          **E** 45 m

**6** One display cabinet holds 38 DVDs.

**How many cabinets will be needed to hold 760 DVDs?**

**A** 18          **B** 16          **C** 19          **D** 20          **E** 17

**7** All the children in Class 6 were asked how many brothers and sisters they have.
The results were recorded in the table below.

| Number of brothers and sisters | Number of children in the class |
|---|---|
| 0 | 3 |
| 1 | 12 |
| 2 | 8 |
| 3 | 1 |

Each child made a card for each of their brothers and sisters.

**How many cards were made?**

**A** 24         **B** 31         **C** 26         **D** 34         **E** 21

---

**8** This bar chart shows the heights of a class of pupils.

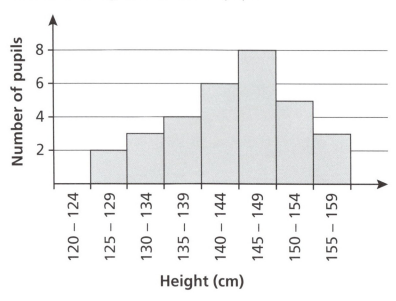

**Which statement MUST be true?**

**A** 2 children are 125 cm tall.

**B** 8 children are at least 140 cm tall, but less than 145 cm tall.

**C** 8 children are more than 144 cm tall, but less than 150 cm tall.

**D** No children are taller than 158 cm.

**E** 4 children are at least 150 cm tall, but less than 160.5 cm tall.

# Practice Paper 4

# Mathematics

**Read the following carefully:**

1. **Do not open or turn over the page in this booklet until you are told to do so.**

2. This is a multiple-choice test in which you have to mark your answer to each question on the separate answer sheet. You should mark only one answer for each question.

3. Draw a firm line clearly through the rectangle next to your answer like this ⟺. If you make a mistake, rub it out as completely as you can and put in your new answer.

4. Be sure to keep your place on the answer sheet. Mark your answer in the box that has the same number as the question.

5. You may not be able to finish all the questions, but try to do as many as you can. If you cannot do a question, **do not waste time on it but go on to the next**. If you are not sure of an answer, choose the one you think is best.

6. You may do any rough working on a separate sheet of paper.

7. **Work as quickly and as carefully as you can.**

8. You will have **50 minutes** to do the test.

# 1

## 3209

### What is this number in words?

- A three thousand two hundred and ninety
- B three thousand two hundred and nine
- C thirty-two thousand and nine
- D three thousand and twenty-nine
- E thirty-two thousand and ninety

# 2

### Which of these words has a vertical line of symmetry?

**BOB**

**HOD**

**TOT**

**KID**

**COOK**

A BOB      B HOD      C TOT      D KID      E COOK

# 3

### How should the time half past six in the evening be written?

A 16:30      B 20:30      C 17:30      D 06:30      E 18:30

**9**  **Which answer is NOT a square number?**

A  16          B  9          C  25          D  36          E  12

---

**10**  There is a number sequence in this magic grid.

| 4 | 8 | 12 |
|---|---|----|
| 8 | ? | 16 |
| 12 | 16 | 20 |

**What is the missing number?**

A  16          B  8          C  4          D  12          E  20

---

**11**

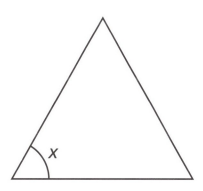

**What is the approximate size of angle *x* inside the triangle?**

A  30°          B  90°          C  120°          D  60°          E  45°

---

**12**  **What fraction of 2.4 litres is 400 ml?**

A  ⅓          B  ³⁄₆          C  ⅛          D  ⅙          E  ²⁄₄

---

**13**

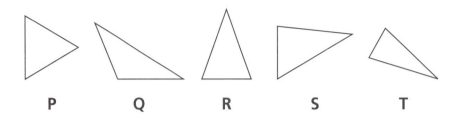

Which triangle has an obtuse angle?

**A** P          **B** Q          **C** R          **D** S          **E** T

**14**

525 raffle tickets were sold by 25 pupils in one school.

If all pupils sold the same number of tickets, how many tickets did each pupil sell?

**A** 41          **B** 31          **C** 21          **D** 19          **E** 20

**15**

How many of the shapes below are trapeziums?

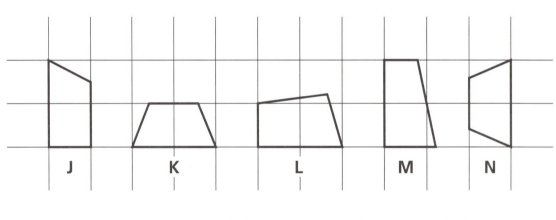

**A** 0          **B** 2          **C** 3          **D** 4          **E** 5

**16**

Look at this number line.

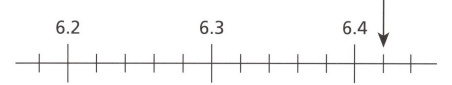

**What number does the arrow point to?**

**A** 6.42      **B** 6.41      **C** 0.02      **D** 6.40      **E** 6.32

**17**

There are 22 boys and 33 girls in the school chess club.

**What fraction of the club is made up of girls?**

**A** $\frac{2}{5}$      **B** $\frac{22}{33}$      **C** $\frac{3}{11}$      **D** $\frac{3}{5}$      **E** $\frac{5}{11}$

**18**

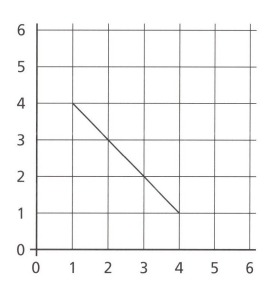

The end points of five lines are shown below.

**Which line is parallel to the line in the diagram?**

**A** (1 , 1) and (4 , 4)
**B** (4 , 1) and (4 , 4)
**C** (2 , 2) and (5 , 5)
**D** (5 , 2) and (2 , 5)
**E** (4 , 1) and (6 , 3)

**19**  Look at this grid in which there are some empty spaces.

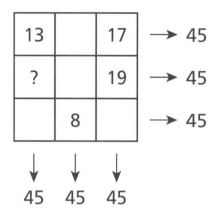

When every square is filled in, each row and each column adds up to 45.

**Which number should be in the square with the question mark?**

A  15          B  28          C  9          D  22          E  4

---

**20**  These shapes are drawn on a centimetre square grid.

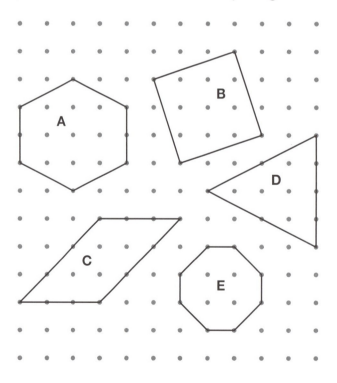

**Which shape has all sides of equal length?**

A  A          B  B          C  C          D  D          E  E

**21** Phoebe enjoys lots of out-of-school activities.
On Sunday she does gymnastics which costs £6.50.
On Tuesday she goes to Brownies which costs £6.
On Wednesday she has a piano lesson which costs £10.
On Thursday she plays the flute in a music group, which costs £7.20.
On Friday she goes to a German class which costs £12.

**What is the total cost of Phoebe's activities each week?**

**A** £31.70      **B** £21.70      **C** £41.70      **D** £35.20      **E** £41.80

**22** In the parallelogram below, angle y measures 110°.

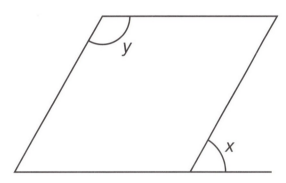

**What is the size of angle x?**

**A** 60°          **B** 70°          **C** 80°          **D** 90°          **E** 110°

**23** In a survey of 85 people, every fifth person had a pierced ear.

**How many people had a pierced ear?**

**A**  0.5 × 85
**B**  85 × $\frac{1}{5}$
**C**  5 ÷ 85
**D**  85 − $\frac{4}{5}$
**E**  85 × 0.25

**24** This table shows the results of a science test:

| Test result | Frequency |
|---|---|
| 16 – 20 | 3 |
| 21 – 25 | 1 |
| 26 – 30 | 5 |
| 31 – 35 | 8 |
| 36 – 40 | 12 |
| 41 – 45 | 11 |
| 46 – 50 | 2 |

**Which one of these statements is true?**

A   43 children were tested altogether.

B   18 children scored less than 36.

C   Less than half of the children scored above 35.

D   38 children scored between 26 and 45.

E   A third of the children scored between 21 and 35.

**25**

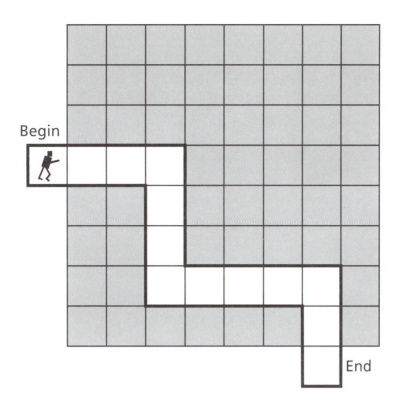

Can you guide the robot along the white squares through this grid?
It starts on the square marked 'Begin' and finishes on the square marked 'End'.
You can only programme it to move FORWARD, TURN LEFT 90° or
TURN RIGHT 90°.

**Which of the instructions below will guide the robot through the grid?**

**A**  FORWARD 3, TURN LEFT 90°, FORWARD 3, TURN RIGHT 90°, FORWARD 4,
TURN LEFT 90°, FORWARD 2.

**B**  FORWARD 4, TURN RIGHT 90°, FORWARD 4, TURN LEFT 90°, FORWARD 4,
TURN RIGHT 90°, FORWARD 2.

**C**  FORWARD 4, TURN RIGHT 90°, FORWARD 3, TURN RIGHT 90°, FORWARD 4,
TURN LEFT 90°, FORWARD 3.

**D**  FORWARD 3, TURN RIGHT 90°, FORWARD 3, TURN RIGHT 90°, FORWARD 4,
TURN RIGHT 90°, FORWARD 2.

**E**  FORWARD 3, TURN RIGHT 90°, FORWARD 3, TURN LEFT 90°, FORWARD 4,
TURN RIGHT 90°, FORWARD 2.

**26**

Rucksacks are being packed into trunks for a hiking trip.
Each trunk holds nine rucksacks.

**How many trunks are needed for 79 rucksacks?**

A 7          B 8          C 9          D 10          E 11

---

**27**

Azara draws a black circle in the middle of a sheet of paper.

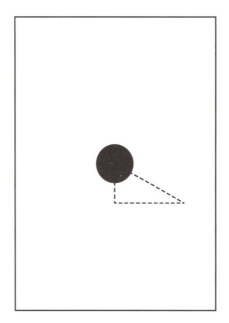

    A          B          C          D          E

She then draws eight triangles of the same shape and size that each have a corner
in the centre of the black circle.
Four of the triangles are displayed in the answer options.

**Which triangle CANNOT be one of the eight?**

A A          B B          C C          D D          E E

**28**

Jonathan gets £4.20 pocket money each week.
His younger brother David gets half as much.

**If David saves all of his pocket money for a whole year, how much money will he have?**

**A** £2.10    **B** £25.20    **C** £52.00    **D** £109.20    **E** £218.40

**29**

Ian is now twice his sister's age.
In four years' time, Ian will be 16.

**How old will his sister be then?**

**A** 6    **B** 7    **C** 16    **D** 12    **E** 10

**30**

**Which of these is the smallest?**

**A** 3.6%    **B** $\frac{1}{25}$    **C** 0.05    **D** 3.49%    **E** $\frac{1}{15}$

**31**

Ella is going on a school holiday which costs £180.
Each week she takes £15 to school towards the cost.
So far she has paid £75.

**How many more weekly payments does she need to make?**

**A** 3    **B** 5    **C** 6    **D** 7    **E** 9

## 32

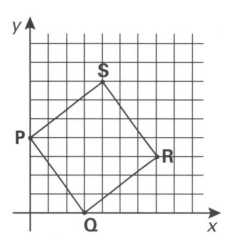

PQRS is a square.

**If the coordinates of point P are (a , b) and point R are (c , d), what is the value of b − d?**

**A** −1          **B** 1          **C** 2          **D** −2          **E** −7

## 33

**How many of the following shapes have at least one pair of parallel sides?**

regular hexagon          regular pentagon          rhombus

isosceles triangle          trapezium

**A** 1          **B** 2          **C** 3          **D** 4          **E** 5

## 34

There are 66 passenger seats on a bus.
The bus left the garage without passengers.
At the first stop, 12 people got on.
At the second stop, 15 people got on.
At the third stop, 19 people got on and 4 got off.
At the fourth stop, 23 people got on and 8 got off.

**How many empty seats are there now?**

**A** 5          **B** 10          **C** 9          **D** 11          **E** 57

**35**

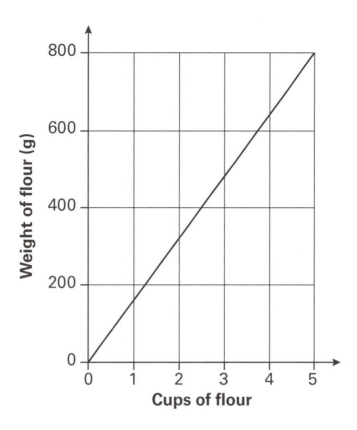

Melissa and Bradley are cooking small cakes for the school bazaar.

The recipe uses cups of flour instead of grams.

Two cups of flour are needed for every egg.

**Use the graph to work out the number of grams of flour they need if they use three eggs?**

**A** 980 g          **B** 900 g          **C** 480 g          **D** 1 kg          **E** 960 g

---

**36**

The perimeter of a rectangle is 18 cm.

**What could be the area of the rectangle?**

**A** 18 cm²          **B** 18 m²          **C** 24 cm²          **D** 81 cm²          **E** 36 cm²

**37**

A stack of 6 identical green boxes weighs the same as a stack of 4 identical yellow boxes.

**Which of the following statements is incorrect?**

A   3 green boxes weigh the same as 2 yellow boxes.
B   8 yellow boxes weigh the same as 12 green boxes.
C   30 green boxes weigh the same as 20 yellow boxes.
D   16 yellow boxes weigh the same as 24 green boxes.
E   36 green boxes weigh the same as 22 yellow boxes.

---

**38**

**Which answer is different from the others?**

A   0.25 of 100
B   25% of 100
C   $\frac{2}{8}$ of 100
D   0.4 of 100
E   $\frac{1}{4}$ of 100

---

**39**

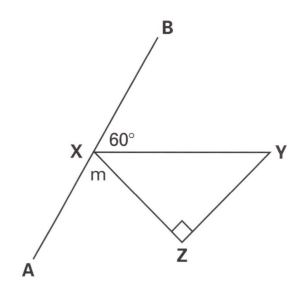

AB is a straight line.
XYZ is an isosceles triangle.

**What size is angle m?**

A  120°          B  95°          C  60°          D  85°          E  75°

**40**

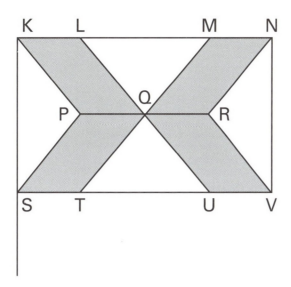

**Which of these pairs of lines is perpendicular?**

A  LU and MT

B  KN and NV

C  PR and TU

D  KP and LQ

E  NR and RV

---

**41**

Two sisters eat Weetbisks cereal for breakfast.

Each Weetbisks box contains 24 biscuits.

Georgina eats $m$ Weetbisks biscuits each morning.

Jennifer is less hungry and has only $n$ Weetbisks biscuits each day.

After four days there are four biscuits left in the Weetbisks box.

**Which answer is correct?**

A  $m = 2$ and $n = 3$

B  $m = 3$ and $n = 2$

C  $m = 3$ and $n = 1$

D  $m = 4$ and $n = 2$

E  $m = 1$ and $n = 4$

**42**

Large cans of lemonade hold 330 ml.

Small cans hold 150 ml.

On Monday, Kerry drank a large can.

On Tuesday she drank two small cans and on Wednesday she drank one small can.

Her younger brother, Sam, drank exactly half the amount that Kerry drank in total.

**How much did Sam drink?**

A  450 ml       B  780 ml       C  480 ml       D  390 ml       E  630 ml

---

**43**

The Class 6 children were asked if they went walking, cycling or swimming during the holidays.

The number of children doing each activity was put on a Venn diagram.

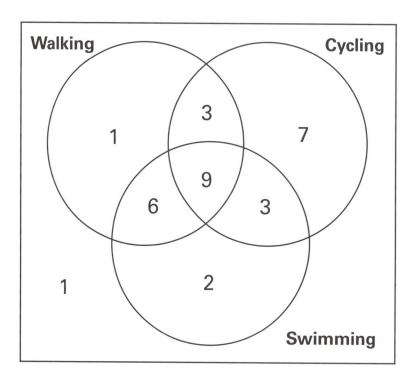

**What fraction of the class did swimming AND cycling?**

A  $^{15}/_{32}$       B  $^{3}/_{32}$       C  $^{15}/_{16}$       D  $^{3}/_{8}$       E  $^{12}/_{31}$

**44**

St Gregory's School held a book fair.

Each book cost £2.99.

250 books were bought by the children altogether.

**What was the total amount of money spent by the children at the fair?**

A   £20.93

B   £74.75

C   £209.30

D   £747.50

E   £2093.00

---

**45**

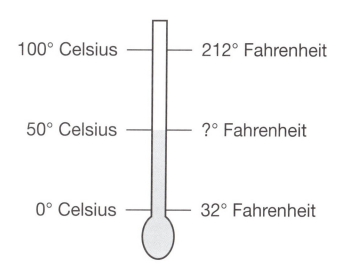

The diagram shows two temperatures in degrees Celsius and in degrees Fahrenheit.

**What is 50 degrees Celsius in degrees Fahrenheit?**

A   50° Fahrenheit

B   106° Fahrenheit

C   122° Fahrenheit

D   148° Fahrenheit

E   162° Fahrenheit

**46** 1 foot is about 0.305 metres and 1 inch is about 0.025 metres.
Patrick is 4 feet 11 inches tall.

**Which is closest to his height in metres?**

**A** 1.3 m          **B** 1.4 m          **C** 1.5 m          **D** 1.6 m          **E** 1.7 m

---

**47** Sam gets £15 pocket money **each month** from his parents.
He also gets £9.50 **each week** from his paper round.

**How much money does Sam get in one year?**

**A** £674          **B** £1568          **C** £894          **D** £1274          **E** £294

---

**48** Joanne's mum and dad run a café.
In summer, fruit salad is very popular.
Every day they use:

       4 kg apples which cost them £2.30 per kg
       6 kg oranges which cost them £3 per kg
       5 kg bananas which cost them £2 per kg
       3 kg grapes which cost them £4 per kg
       2 kg strawberries which cost them £3.50 per kg

**How much is their daily fruit bill?**

**A** £14.80          **B** £56.20          **C** £27.20          **D** £49.20          **E** £51.80

**49**  **Which answer has the greatest value?**

A  20% of 220

B  ½ of 220

C  ²/₁₀ of 220

D  102

E  0.2 of 220

---

**50**

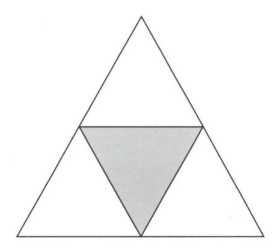

The area of the shaded triangle is 250 mm².

**What is the area of the large triangle?**

A  750 mm²

B  50 cm²

C  10 cm²

D  250 cm²

E  75 cm²

End of Test

Published by GL Assessment, 1st Floor, Vantage London, Great West Road, Brentford TW8 9AG.

Printed in China.

Code 6802 026
1(11.18) PF

# Practice Paper 5

# Mathematics

**Read the following carefully:**

1. **Do not open or turn over the page in this booklet until you are told to do so.**

2. This is a multiple-choice test in which you have to mark your answer to each question on the separate answer sheet. You should mark only one answer for each question.

3. Draw a firm line clearly through the rectangle next to your answer like this ▭. If you make a mistake, rub it out as completely as you can and put in your new answer.

4. Be sure to keep your place on the answer sheet. Mark your answer in the box that has the same number as the question.

5. You may not be able to finish all the questions, but try to do as many as you can. If you cannot do a question, **do not waste time on it but go on to the next**. If you are not sure of an answer, choose the one you think is best.

6. You may do any rough working on a separate sheet of paper.

7. **Work as quickly and as carefully as you can.**

8. You will have **50 minutes** to do the test.

**1** Meera made this shape from straws.

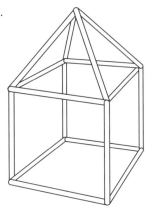

She wants to make the same shape from tiles like these.

**What tiles does she need?**

**A** 4 squares and 3 triangles

**B** 4 squares and 4 triangles

**C** 4 squares and 5 triangles

**D** 5 squares and 4 triangles

**E** 5 squares and 5 triangles

---

**2** Last year, the sales for a shopping centre were nine million, ninety-two thousand and forty-five pounds.

**What is this in figures?**

**A** £9 920 450

**B** £9 092 045

**C** £9 009 245

**D** £9 092 450

**E** £9 920 045

**3**

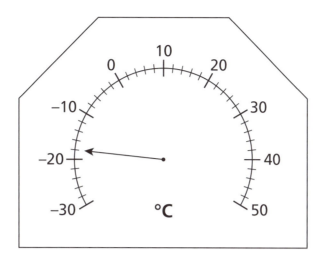

The dial shows the temperature inside a freezer.

**What is the temperature in the freezer?**

**A** −19 °C     **B** −22 °C     **C** −14 °C     **D** −21 °C     **E** −18 °C

**4**

Hannah made some biscuits for a party.
She put them all out on plates.
Each plate has the same number of biscuits.

**How many biscuits could Hannah have made?**

**A** 13     **B** 17     **C** 19     **D** 21     **E** 23

**5**

Some pupils recorded the numbers of different types of bird that they saw at a bird table.
The bar chart shows their results.

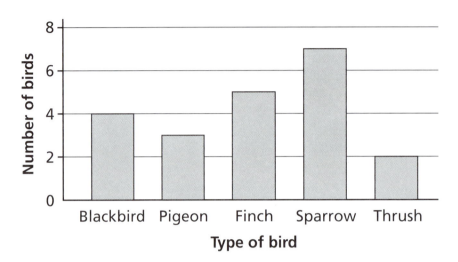

**How many more finches than thrushes did they see?**

**A** 1      **B** 2      **C** 3      **D** 4      **E** 5

**6**

Karen, Amrit and Sam are going to share two pizzas equally between them.

**What fraction of a whole pizza should each of them have?**

**A** ½      **B** ¾      **C** ¼      **D** ⅓      **E** ⅔

**7**

Dinesh spends £1.13.
He pays with a £2 coin.

**What is the smallest number of coins that he can receive in change?**

**A** 6 **B** 7 **C** 4 **D** 5 **E** 8

---

**8**

**What number should go in the box?**

$$1680 + 1680 + 1680 + 1680 + 1680 = \boxed{\phantom{0000}} \times 10$$

**A** 84 **B** 336 **C** 840 **D** 420 **E** 168

---

**9**

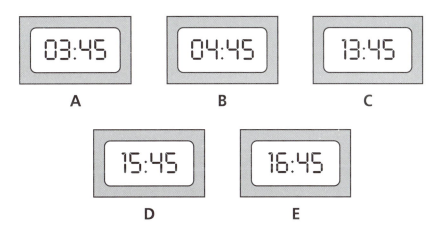

A     B     C

D     E

**Which of these digital clocks shows that it is a quarter to four in the afternoon?**

**A** A **B** B **C** C **D** D **E** E

---

**10** Here is part of a railway timetable.

| London Paddington to Bath Spa | | | | | |
| --- | --- | --- | --- | --- | --- |
| **London Paddington** | 0527 | 0630 | 0645 | 0700 | 0715 |
| **Reading** | 0557 | 0657 | 0711 | 0727 | 0741 |
| **Didcot Parkway** | | 0712 | | 0742 | 0756 |
| **Swindon** | 0625 | 0730 | 0740 | 0800 | 0815 |
| **Chippenham** | 0640 | 0745 | | 0815 | |
| **Bath Spa** | 0653 | 0800 | | 0830 | |

Maya wants to arrive in Didcot Parkway by half past seven in the morning.

**What time must she leave London Paddington?**

A  0527        B  0630        C  0645        D  0700        E  0712

**11**  **What is the cost of eight mugs at £1.99 each?**

A  £15.92

B  £15.98

C  £16.00

D  £16.02

E  £16.08

**12**   Look at the Venn diagram.

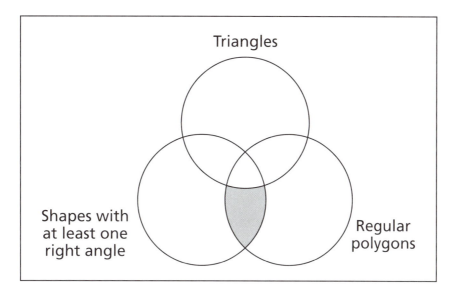

**Which of these shapes should go into the shaded region?**

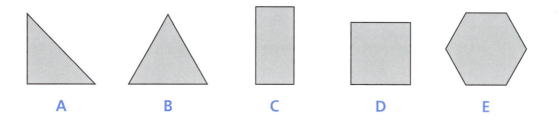

A          B          C          D          E

**13**   **What is 1 – 0.11?**

A  0.99          B  0.09          C  0.91          D  0.19          E  0.89

**14**  This shape is drawn on triangle dotty paper.

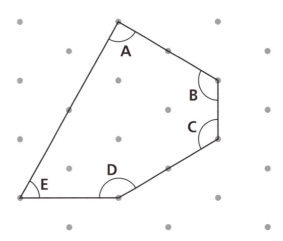

**One of the angles is 60°. Which one is it?**

**A** A          **B** B          **C** C          **D** D          **E** E

---

**15**  This repeating pattern is made up of squares, triangles and circles.

The pattern repeats after five shapes.
It goes on and on, repeating again and again.

**What fraction of all the shapes in the pattern are squares?**

**A** $\frac{1}{5}$          **B** $\frac{1}{2}$          **C** $\frac{2}{5}$          **D** $\frac{6}{10}$          **E** $\frac{6}{13}$

**16**

Five friends were all born in 2007.
Their birthdays are shown in the table below.

| Child | Birthday |
|---|---|
| Kieran | 3rd July |
| Haq | 31st May |
| Harriet | 16th June |
| Lisa | 10th May |
| Jake | 28th July |

**Who is the oldest?**

**A** Kieran          **B** Haq          **C** Harriet          **D** Lisa          **E** Jake

---

**17**

Akira wants to calculate the cost of:
two teas, one coffee, two sandwiches and three apples.

> **Café**
> Tea or coffee........ £1.99
> Juice ..................... £1.49
> Sandwich.............. £2.99
> Doughnut ............ £1.49
> Apple...................... 49p

**Which of these calculations could he do?**

**A**  $3 \times £2 + 2 \times £3 + 3 \times 50p + 3p$

**B**  $3 \times £2 + 2 \times £3 + 3 \times 50p - 4p$

**C**  $3 \times £2 + 2 \times £3 + 3 \times 50p + 4p$

**D**  $3 \times £2 + 2 \times £3 + 3 \times 50p + 8p$

**E**  $3 \times £2 + 2 \times £3 + 3 \times 50p - 8p$

**18**  These four shapes are drawn on a triangle dotty grid.

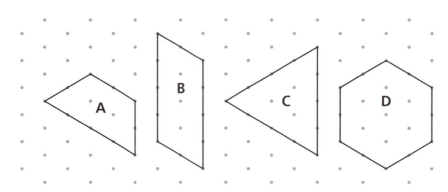

**Which two shapes have the same area?**

**A**  A and B          **B**  B and C          **C**  C and D          **D**  A and C          **E**  B and D

**19**  **Which of these statements is correct?**

**A**  $4\frac{1}{5} < 4.5$

**B**  $4\frac{1}{2} < 4.5$

**C**  $4\frac{1}{5} > 4.5$

**D**  $4\frac{1}{2} > 4.5$

**E**  $4\frac{1}{5} = 4.5$

**20**  10 pupils picked blackberries.
The table shows how many kilograms of blackberries they picked.

| Weight in kilograms | Number of pupils |
|---|---|
| Less than ½ kg | 2 |
| ½ kg to less than 1 kg | 0 |
| 1 kg to less than 1½ kg | 4 |
| 1½ kg to less than 2 kg | 3 |
| 2 kg to less than 2½ kg | 1 |

**How many pupils picked at least 1 kilogram?**

**A**  0          **B**  4          **C**  6          **D**  8          **E**  10

**21**

$37 \times 497 + 63 \times 497 =$

**A** 9443

**B** 44 730

**C** 49 700

**D** 54 670

**E** 9 170 644

---

**22**

This is the front view of a large building.

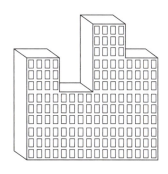

**Which is the rear view of the building?**

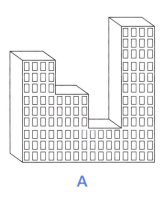

**A**

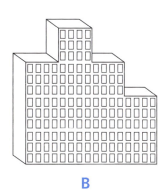

**B**

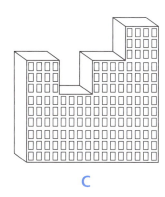

**C**

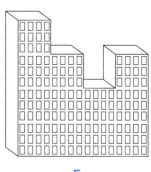

**D**

**E**

**23**

Josh started from a number between 1 and 5, and counted on in steps of 6.
He reached the number 22.

**What number did he start from?**

**A** 4          **B** 2          **C** 1          **D** 3          **E** 5

---

**24**

Callum is facing south-east.
He can see a tree in front of him, and a house on his left.

**Which map is he on?**

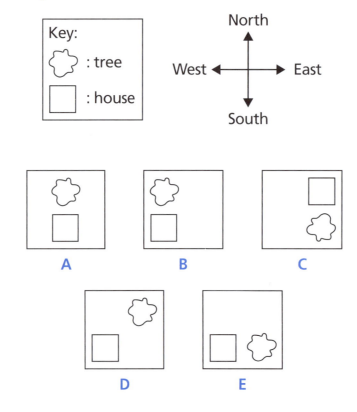

---

**25**

There are 816 pupils at Southfields School.
There are 28 more girls than boys in the school.

**How many girls are there in the school?**

**A** 380          **B** 436          **C** 408          **D** 394          **E** 422

**26**

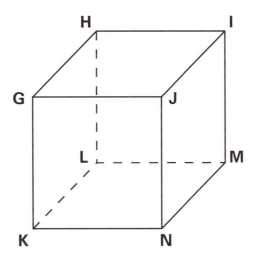

A cube has vertices G, H, I, J, K, L, M and N.
A cut is made through the plane GJML.

**Which name best describes the cut face GJML?**

**A** square     **B** rectangle     **C** rhombus     **D** quadrilateral     **E** trapezium

**27**

Look at the information about what is in 100 grams of dried pasta.

| 100 g contains: | |
|---|---|
| Protein | 14.4 g |
| Carbohydrate | 66.4 g |
| Fat | 3.5 g |
| Fibre | 2.6 g |

**How many grams of protein are there in 1 kilogram of pasta?**

**A** 1.44 g     **B** 0.144 g     **C** 144 g     **D** 86.9 g     **E** 1.44 kg

**28**   Five pupils played a game and scored points four times.
The graph shows how many points each pupil scored in each game.

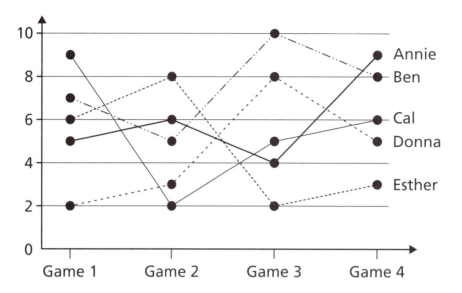

**Which pupil had the greatest difference between their lowest and highest scores?**

**A** Annie          **B** Ben          **C** Cal          **D** Donna          **E** Esther

**29**   The sum of the first four square numbers is 30.

**What is the sum of the first five square numbers?**

**A** 55          **B** 35          **C** 25          **D** 45          **E** 65

**30**

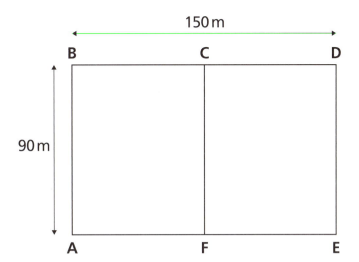

The playing field of Freeborough Primary School is a rectangle 150 metres long by 90 metres wide.

C and F are the middle points of the long sides.

The pupils are taking part in a sponsored walk around the field.

For each lap, the juniors walk around the rectangle ABDE and back to A.

For each lap, the infants walk around the rectangle ABCF and back to A.

**How much further do the juniors walk than the infants for each lap?**

**A** 75 m        **B** 150 m        **C** 240 m        **D** 300 m        **E** 330 m

---

**31**

**What number is the arrow pointing to on this number line?**

**A** 44.5        **B** 47.05        **C** 47.5        **D** 47.65        **E** 53.5

---

**32** This is a graph that converts cups of flour to grams:

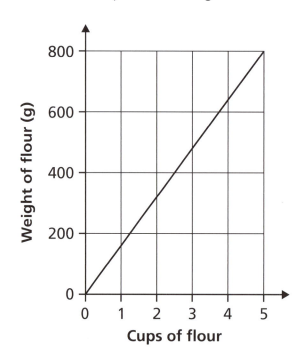

**Use the graph to work out the equivalent amount of flour in grams for 10 cups?**

**A** 800 g          **B** 1050 g          **C** 1250 g          **D** 1500 g          **E** 1600 g

---

**33** Look at this number fact:

789 × 36 = 28 404

**What is 18 × 789?**

**A** 7101          **B** 14 202          **C** 14 204          **D** 14 991          **E** 15 774

# 34

| Gymnastics Test | |
|---|---|
| Activity | Maximum Mark |
| Acrobatics | 30 |
| Balance | 25 |
| Climbing | 25 |

There is a test to enter a gymnastics competition.

Pupils need to score 75% or more in the test.

Zach scored 24 in Acrobatics and 16 in Balance.

He passed the test.

**What was the minimum that he could have scored in the Climbing activity?**

A  20          B  16          C  19          D  15          E  21

# 35

An electric light uses $1\frac{1}{2}$ pence worth of electricity every two hours.

The light is left on from 6 pm on Friday until 6 pm on Sunday.

**How much does the electricity cost?**

A  36p          B  24p          C  12p          D  48p          E  18p

**36**

Jamie had a lot of different coins in his money box.
He sorted them by type of coin.
He counted the number of coins in each group.
He drew a pictogram to show the results.

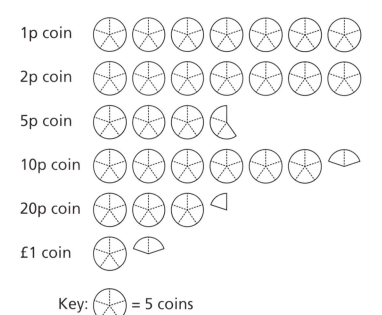

1p coin

2p coin

5p coin

10p coin

20p coin

£1 coin

Key: = 5 coins

**Which two groups of coins had the same value?**

A   1p and 2p
B   2p and 5p
C   5p and 10p
D   10p and 20p
E   20p and £1

---

**37**

A two-litre bottle of fruit squash is mixed with four times as much water.

**How many 125-millilitre cups can be filled with the diluted squash?**

A  20          B  80          C  64          D  100          E  40

**38**

Bulu has a 2D shape.
All of its sides are the same length.

**Which of these CANNOT be Bulu's shape?**

A  a right-angled triangle

B  an equilateral triangle

C  a square

D  a rectangle

E  a parallelogram

**39**

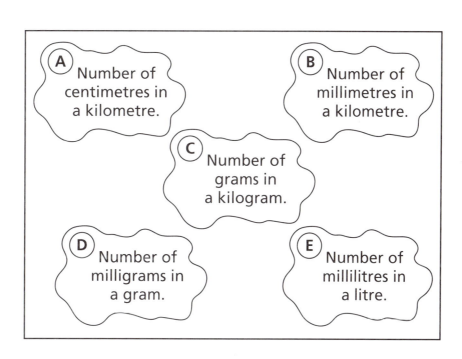

**Which one of these is equal to one million?**

A  A          B  B          C  C          D  D          E  E

**40**

The price of a television is reduced in a sale by 20%.

**If the sale price is £160, what was the original price of the television?**

A  £128          B  £180          C  £200          D  £192          E  £188

**41**  Mrs Rai buys five metres of ribbon.
She cuts off three equal pieces and has 20 cm left.

**What is the length of each of the three pieces?**

A  480 cm        B  1.6 cm        C  250 cm        D  320 cm        E  160 cm

**42**

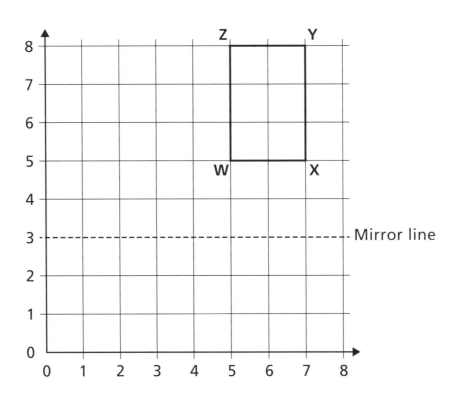

The rectangle WXYZ is reflected in the mirror line.

**What will the new coordinates of point X be?**

A  (7 , 1)        B  (7 , 2)        C  (5 , 1)        D  (2 , 7)        E  (7 , 3)

**43** The numbers on the opposite faces of a number cube always add up to 7.

**Which of these nets will fold up to make a number cube?**

| A | B | C | D | E |
|---|---|---|---|---|
| 5 | 3 | 1 | 4 | 2 |
| 6 1 3 | 6 5 1 | 4 2 5 | 5 2 1 | 6 3 1 |
| 2 | 2 | 6 | 3 | 5 |
| 4 | 4 | 3 | 6 | 4 |

**44** This advertisement is misleading.

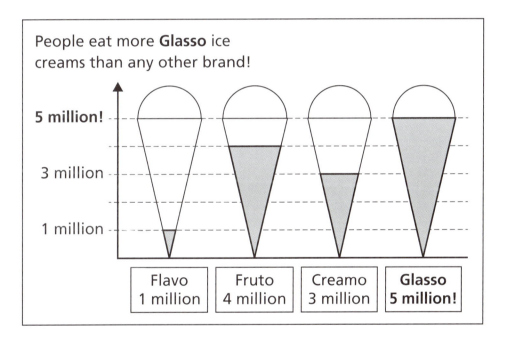

People eat more **Glasso** ice creams than any other brand!

| Flavo | Fruto | Creamo | Glasso |
|---|---|---|---|
| 1 million | 4 million | 3 million | 5 million! |

**Why is it misleading?**

A   The ice cream cones are unevenly spaced along the horizontal axis.

B   The values along the vertical axis are unevenly spaced.

C   The area for Glasso is more than five times the area for Flavo.

D   It does not show how many will be sold next year.

E   It does not show how many ice lollies or sweets people eat.

**45**

Cinema tickets for adults cost £10.20.
Children's tickets are half price.

**In pounds, how much do the tickets cost for a group of five adults and 10 children?**

**A** £51     **B** £102     **C** £5.10     **D** £127.50     **E** £25.50

---

**46**

Rosie draws a square on a coordinate grid with corners at (5 , 5), (7 , 5), (7 , 7) and (5 , 7).

**Which one of these points is inside Rosie's square?**

**A** (4 , 4)     **B** (6 , 6)     **C** (6 , 8)     **D** (8 , 8)     **E** (4 , 6)

---

**47**

The distance around the outside of Fran's bicycle is 150 cm.

150 cm

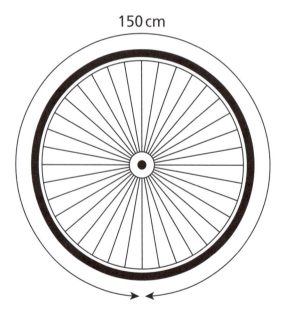

**How many complete revolutions must the wheel make for Fran to travel 1.5 km?**

**A** 1000     **B** 100     **C** 10 000     **D** 100 000     **E** 10

**48**

This shows some angles on a diagram of an iron gate.

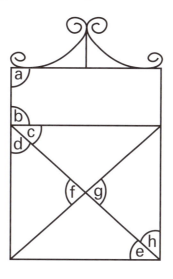

**Which of these is not necessarily true?**

**A** a = b          **B** d = h          **C** a = c + d      **D** e = h          **E** f = g

---

**49**

Look at this number machine.

N ⟶ | ÷ 4 | ⟶ | + 1 | ⟶ | × 2 | ⟶ ?

**If Nilesh ended up with the number 4, what number did he start with?**

**A** 2          **B** 6          **C** 4          **D** 8          **E** 1

---

**50**

A tin of paint costs £6 and will cover five square metres of wall.

**What is the cost of paint tins for a wall 4.5 m long and 3 m high?**

**A** £12          **B** £13.50          **C** £15          **D** £16.20          **E** £18

Published by GL Assessment, 1st Floor, Vantage London, Great West Road, Brentford TW8 9AG.

Printed in China.

Code 6802 027
1(11.18) PF

# Practice Paper 6

# Mathematics

**Read the following carefully:**

1. **Do not open or turn over the page in this booklet until you are told to do so.**

2. This is a multiple-choice test in which you have to mark your answer to each question on the separate answer sheet. You should mark only one answer for each question.

3. Draw a firm line clearly through the rectangle next to your answer like this ▭. If you make a mistake, rub it out as completely as you can and put in your new answer.

4. Be sure to keep your place on the answer sheet. Mark your answer in the box that has the same number as the question.

5. You may not be able to finish all the questions, but try to do as many as you can. If you cannot do a question, **do not waste time on it but go on to the next**. If you are not sure of an answer, choose the one you think is best.

6. You may do any rough working on a separate sheet of paper.

7. **Work as quickly and as carefully as you can.**

8. You will have **50 minutes** to do the test.

## 1

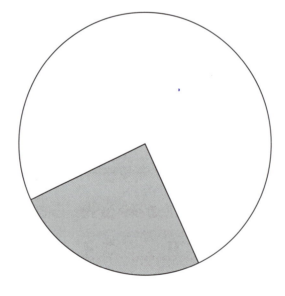

Look at this shape drawn on a squares grid.

**How many lines of symmetry does the shape have?**

**A** 4         **B** 1         **C** 8         **D** 6         **E** 2

---

## 2

**What fraction of the circle is shaded?**

**A** ¹⁄₂       **B** ¹⁄₃       **C** ¹⁄₄       **D** ¹⁄₅       **E** ¹⁄₆

**3**

| City | Temperature (°C) |
|------|------------------|
| Beijing | −6 |
| Cape Town | 16 |
| Helsinki | −14 |
| London | 4 |
| Mumbai | 24 |

**Which two cities have a difference in temperature of 10 degrees?**

A   Beijing and Cape Town

B   Beijing and London

C   Cape Town and Helsinki

D   Helsinki and London

E   Helsinki and Mumbai

**4**

These numbers go round in a spiral.

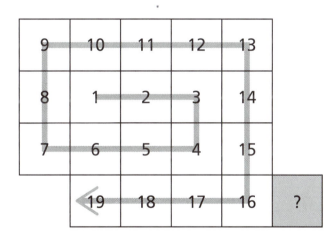

The spiral goes on.

**What number will be to the right of 16 in the spiral?**

A 31          B 32          C 33          D 34          E 35

**5** Harri has two T-shapes each made out of four squares.

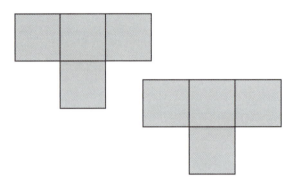

He fits them together to make another shape.

**Which shape can Harri make?**

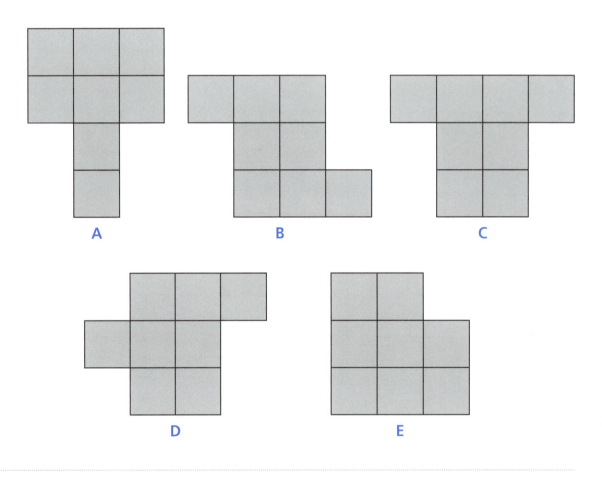

A          B          C

D          E

---

**6** **What is 13.83 + 4.5?**

A 14.28          B 18.33          C 18.3          D 18.88          E 17.33

**7** Estimate the size of this angle.

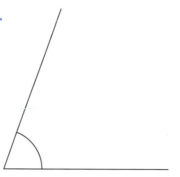

**A** 10°  **B** 30°  **C** 50°  **D** 70°  **E** 90°

**8** Which of these sets of coins has the greatest value?

**A**

**B**

**C**

**D**

**E**

**9**

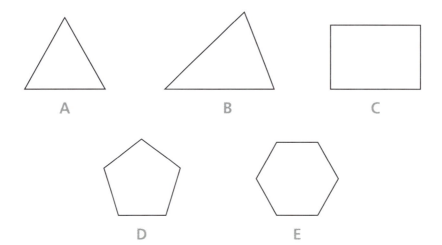

A

B

C

D

E

Four of these shapes will fit together with shapes of the same kind, without leaving any gaps.

**Which one will NOT?**

**A** A          **B** B          **C** C          **D** D          **E** E

---

**10**

A company ordered three cartons of pencils on Monday and seven cartons on Tuesday.
Each carton contained 144 pencils.

**How many pencils did the company order altogether?**

**A** 1008          **B** 3024          **C** 1152          **D** 1011          **E** 1440

**11**

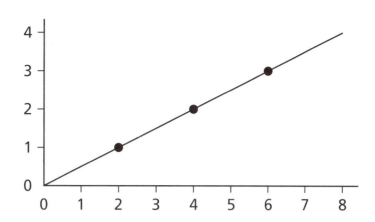

Three points on this line have been plotted at (2 , 1), (4 , 2) and (6 , 3).

**Using the same pattern, what are the coordinates of the 10th point?**

**A** (10 , 5)     **B** (5 , 10)     **C** (20 , 10)     **D** (10 , 20)     **E** (15 , 10)

---

**12**     **What percentage of this regular octagon is shaded?**

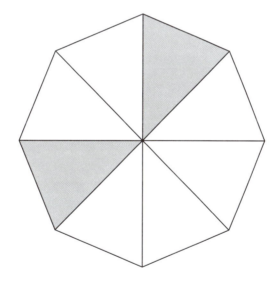

**A** 10%     **B** 15%     **C** 20%     **D** 25%     **E** 30%

**13** This gate is made of seven planks of wood.

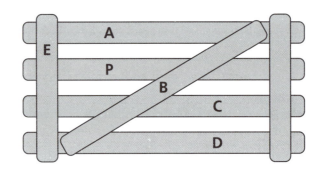

**Which plank is perpendicular to plank P?**

**A** A      **B** B      **C** C      **D** D      **E** E

**14** Mrs Lee has 212 exercise books.
She packs them into boxes of 30.

**How many exercise books does she have left over?**

**A** 2      **B** 4      **C** 6      **D** 8      **E** 10

**15** Two of the labels are missing from this sorting diagram.

|           | ?        | ?        |
|-----------|----------|----------|
| Prime     |          | 2   3    |
|           |          | 5     7  |
| Not prime | 1   4    | 6        |
|           |     9    |       8  |

**Which of these are the missing labels?**

**A**  Odd; Even

**B**  Less than 5; 5 or more

**C**  Prime; Not prime

**D**  Square; Not square

**E**  Whole numbers; Not whole numbers

**16** Three pumpkins weigh 13.2 kg, 7.6 kg and 11.4 kg.

**What is the total weight of the pumpkins?**

**A** 32.2 kg    **B** 22.2 kg    **C** 31.2 kg    **D** 21.2 kg    **E** 33.2 kg

**17** Harpreet wants to measure the area of a photograph in a magazine.

**What units should he use?**

**A** metres

**B** square metres

**C** centimetres

**D** millimetres

**E** square centimetres

**18** A poster said:

*It takes*
**300 kilograms of coal**
*to run a*
**100-watt bulb**
**24 hours a day**
*for a year.*

***That's equal***
***to the weight of***
***three baby elephants!***

**How many 100-watt light bulbs could you run for 12 hours a day for a year with 1200 kilograms of coal?**

**A** 2    **B** 4    **C** 6    **D** 8    **E** 10

**19**  Anita has the following five shapes.

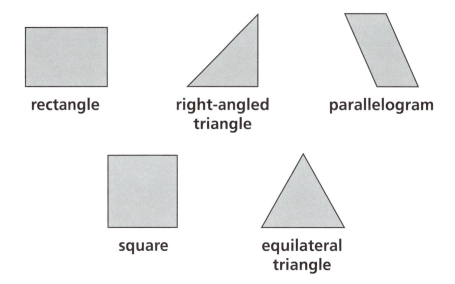

**rectangle**    **right-angled triangle**    **parallelogram**

**square**    **equilateral triangle**

She uses a sorting diagram to sort her shapes.

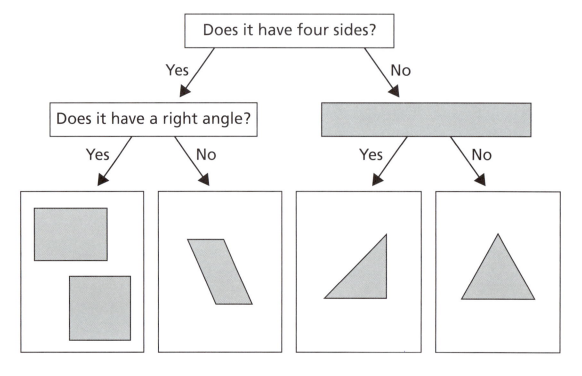

**Which of these should be in the shaded box?**

A  Does it have a right angle?

B  Does it have fewer than four sides?

C  Are all its sides equal?

D  Does it have two right angles?

E  Is it a triangle?

**20**  **Which of these statements is always true?**

A  If a number ends in a four then it must be a multiple of four.

B  If the sum of all the digits in a number is a multiple of four then the number must be a multiple of four.

C  If the last two digits in a number are a multiple of four then the number must be a multiple of four.

D  If there are at least two fours in a number then it must be a multiple of four.

E  If a number is even then it must be a multiple of four.

**21**  Look at this shape.

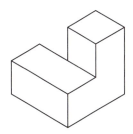

**Which one of these is the same shape turned around?**

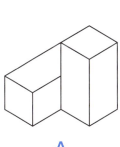

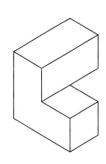

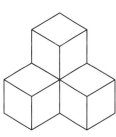

A                    B                    C

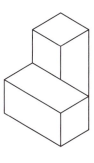

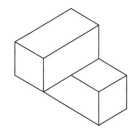

D                    E

**22**

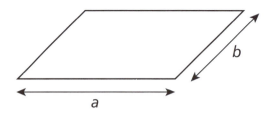

What is the formula for the perimeter of this parallelogram?

**A** $a + b$      **B** $2a + 2b$      **C** $a \times b$      **D** $a \times 2b$      **E** $2a \times 2b$

---

**23**

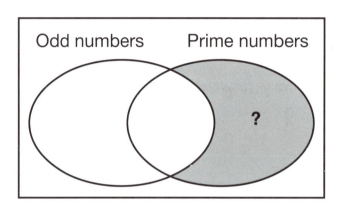

Which of these numbers should go in the shaded area on the Venn diagram?

**A** 2      **B** 3      **C** 4      **D** 5      **E** 6

---

**24**

What is the number marked X on this number line?

**A** 25      **B** 35      **C** 45      **D** 55      **E** 65

**25** Misa went to the leisure centre.
She used the gym for 50 minutes and then went swimming for 25 minutes.

**How long did she exercise altogether?**

A  1 hour and 15 minutes

B  1.15 hours

C  7 hours and 5 minutes

D  7.5 hours

E  7 hours and 50 minutes

**26** Two apples and one orange cost £1. One orange costs 40p.

**What is the cost of one apple?**

A  60p          B  20p          C  40p          D  50p          E  30p

**27**

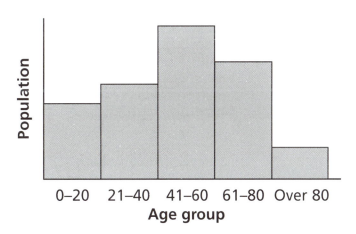

The bar chart shows the population of a town by age group.

**Which of these age groups have about the same population as the 41–60 age group?**

A  0 to 20

B  21 to 40

C  40 and under

D  over 60

E  61 to 80

## 28

$73 - 2\boxed{\phantom{0}} = \boxed{\phantom{0}}9$

Gemma's calculator displays the sum entered and the answer.
The calculator works correctly except that one digit always appears as a blank space.

**What is the missing digit?**

A 3          B 4          C 5          D 6          E 7

## 29

Look at the three triangles below.

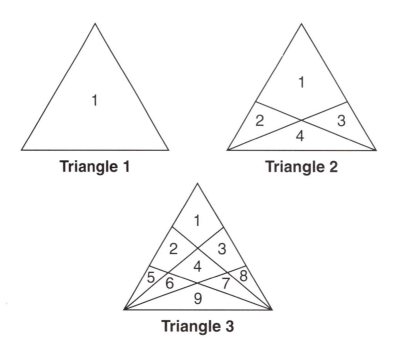

Triangle 1                    Triangle 2

Triangle 3

There are nine shapes in Triangle 3.

**How many shapes will there be in Triangle 4?**

A 36          B 14          C 16          D 25          E 12

**30** Catrin started from the number 12 and counted back in steps of 5.

**Which of these numbers did she count?**

A 0          B −4          C −2          D −1          E −3

---

**31** A swimming club has 50 members.
The table shows some information about them.

|  | Girls | Boys | Total |
|---|---|---|---|
| Left-handed | 2 |  | 6 |
| Right-handed |  |  |  |
| **Total** | **22** |  |  |

**How many members of the club are right-handed boys?**

A 24          B 20          C 4          D 22          E 28

---

**32** $65 \times 320 = 20\ 800$

**What is 6.5 × 3.2?**

A 0.28          B 2.08          C 20.8          D 28          E 208

---

**33** On 1st January 2012, Mr Smith started saving £1 every day.

**In which year had he saved £1000?**

A 2013          B 2014          C 2015          D 2016          E 2017

---

Please go on to the next page >>>

**34**

A pack of five peaches costs £2.50.
A pack of six apples costs £1.50.
Lucy needs 30 peaches and 30 apples.

**How much does she pay?**

**A** £24.00      **B** £21.50      **C** £22.00      **D** £20.00      **E** £22.50

---

**35**

Steve and Ramesh walked from Sildown to Northmere.
They stopped in Northmere for a time and then walked back to Sildown.
The graph shows their journey.

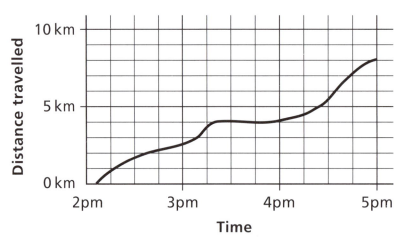

**What is the distance from Sildown to Northmere?**

**A** 2 km      **B** 4 km      **C** 6 km      **D** 8 km      **E** 10 km

**36** **If 30th April is a Wednesday, what day of the week will 30th May be?**

A Friday

B Saturday

C Thursday

D Sunday

E Monday

---

**37** The table below shows the maximum and minimum temperatures for one week in January.

|  | Maximum | Minimum |
|---|---|---|
| Monday | 7°C | 0°C |
| Tuesday | 8°C | –3°C |
| Wednesday | 10°C | 1°C |
| Thursday | 8°C | –4°C |
| Friday | 6°C | –2°C |

**Which day shows the greatest difference between minimum and maximum temperatures?**

A Monday

B Tuesday

C Wednesday

D Thursday

E Friday

---

**38** One 5p coin weighs $3\frac{1}{4}$ grams.

Toby has 40 pence worth of 5p coins.

**How many grams do they weigh?**

A 13    B $16\frac{1}{4}$    C 26    D 52    E 130

---

Please go on to the next page >>>

**39** Shazia counted out one kilogram of each of four different types of potato.
She counted out 32 potatoes in total.
The bar chart shows her results for three of the types of potato.

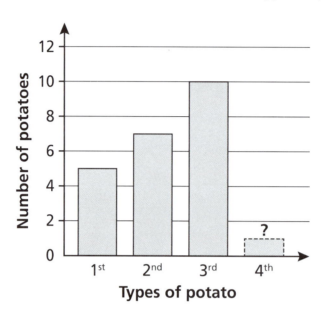

**How many potatoes of the 4th type did Shazia count out?**

A  8          B  9          C  10          D  11          E  12

**40** $32 \div 2 < x^2$

**Which of these numbers is the smallest number $x$ could be?**

A  1          B  2          C  3          D  4          E  5

**41**

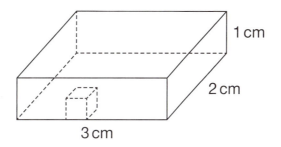

1 cm

2 cm

3 cm

**What is the largest number of cubes of side 0.5 cm that will fit into the cuboid above?**

**A** 48          **B** 12          **C** 24          **D** 6          **E** 96

---

**42**

**Which of these pairs of numbers are equally distant from 3?**

**A**  3.01 and 2.91
**B**  3.01 and 2.99
**C**  3.11 and 2.91
**D**  3.11 and 2.99
**E**  3.19 and 2.91

---

**43**

The original price of a backpack was £81.
During a sale, the price of the backpack was reduced by £4.50 each week.

**After how many weeks would the price of the backpack be ⅝ of the original price?**

**A** 9          **B** 11          **C** 16          **D** 8          **E** 10

---

**44**

In a town, 15% of total household waste is recycled.
30 000 tonnes are recycled.

**How many tonnes are NOT recycled?**

**A** 45 000          **B** 30 000          **C** 200 000          **D** 55 000          **E** 170 000

---

## 45

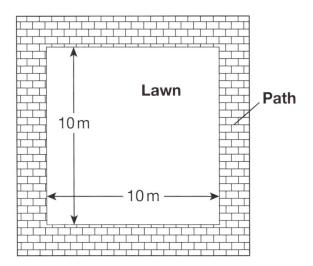

The figure shows a 10 metre by 10 metre lawn surrounded by a path 2 metres wide.

**What is the outer perimeter of the path?**

**A** 40 m          **B** 42 m          **C** 48 m          **D** 52 m          **E** 56 m

## 46

The diagram shows a square drawn on a square coordinate grid.

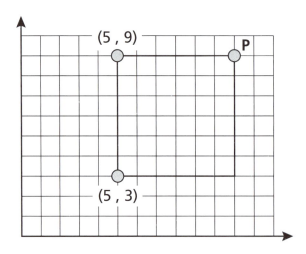

**What are the coordinates of point P?**

**A** (9 , 11)          **B** (10 , 12)          **C** (10 , 9)          **D** (11 , 9)          **E** (11 , 15)

**47**

Adam sleeps nine hours a night for five nights a week, and 11 hours for two nights a week.

**Which is closest to the percentage of the whole week that Adam spends sleeping?**

**A** 25%  **B** 30%  **C** 33%  **D** 40%  **E** 50%

---

**48**

Look at the results of the 150-metre race.

**Who came first in the race?**

| Name | Time |
|------|------|
| Adi | 32.7 seconds |
| Bethan | 32.75 seconds |
| Carlos | 32.57 seconds |
| Danny | 32.71 seconds |
| Ella | 32.07 seconds |

**A** Adi  **B** Bethan  **C** Carlos  **D** Danny  **E** Ella

**49**

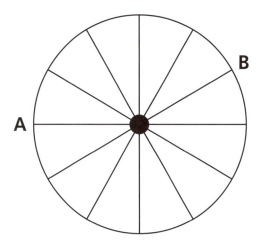

This circle is divided into 12 equal sectors.

**What is the smaller angle between point A and point B?**

**A** 110°        **B** 150°        **C** 120°        **D** 210°        **E** 30°

---

**50**

A shirt costs £12.30.
The price is reduced by $\frac{1}{3}$.

**Which one of these is the lowest amount you need to buy it?**

**A** £4        **B** £5        **C** £7        **D** £8        **E** £9

Published by GL Assessment, 1st Floor, Vantage London, Great West Road, Brentford TW8 9AG.

Printed in China.

Code 6802 028
1(11.18) PF

# Notes and Answers for Parents

# Mathematics
# Pack 2

# Introduction

## About the Tests

These tests are designed to give your child practice in sitting a formal type of examination before they take the actual 11+ test.

The papers are presented in a very similar way to many of the test papers used for selection at 11+, and the questions represent the type of questions used, although they may not be exactly the same level of difficulty. Therefore, your child's scores on these tests will not necessarily be a direct indication of their likely score on an actual 11+ test. Furthermore, the pass marks for the actual test will depend, to some extent, on the overall standard of the candidates.

## Preparation for Testing

Give your child the test at an appropriate time, when they are both physically and mentally alert. Choose a suitable area for them to work in – make sure they can work comfortably and are free from any distractions.

Before your child takes a practice test, discuss with them the reasons why they are doing the test. Also, explain that they might find some of the questions difficult, but that they should work as quickly and as carefully as they can. If they get stuck on a question, they should not waste too much time on it but move on to the next one. If they have time left at the end, they can go back to it then.

# Taking the Tests

Your child should record their answers in the Answer Sheets booklet provided – not in the test booklet. Answer Sheets are provided for all three tests in this pack.

The actual 11+ test will be marked by a computer, but you will need to score the practice tests yourself using the Answer Key in this booklet. It is important for your child to learn how to use the Answer Sheets properly, in preparation for the real test: they should record an answer in the appropriate box by drawing a clear line through it with a pencil. Mistakes should be rubbed out carefully and **not** crossed out, since in the actual test this would not be recorded correctly by the computer. You can ignore the boxes at the top marked 'Pupil Number', 'School Number' and 'Date of Birth'. These need to be filled in only for the actual test. By encountering these features now, your child will be more familiar with the style of the actual 11+ paper when they take the test.

### Timing a Test
It is useful for your child to practise taking tests under timed conditions. Allow them 50 minutes for a test, but do not start timing until they have read all the instructions and/or filled in all the details at the top of the Answer Sheet.

If they have not finished at the end of 50 minutes, draw a line underneath the question they are on, or draw a ring around its number, and then let them carry on. When you mark the test, you will be able to see how many questions your child got right in the allocated time and how many questions overall. This will give you a good indication of whether they need to develop their speed and/or work more accurately.

# Marking and Feedback

The answers are provided on pages 4–6. Only these answers are allowed. One mark should be given for each correct answer – do not allow half marks or 'the benefit of the doubt'. Do not deduct marks for wrong answers.

The results may suggest that more practice is needed. Always try to be positive and encouraging. Talk through the mistakes your child has made in a constructive way. Work out together how to get the right answer.

# Answer Key

**Practice Paper 4**

| Question | Answer | Question | Answer | Question | Answer |
|---|---|---|---|---|---|
| 1 | B | 21 | £41.70 | 41 | $m = 3$ and $n = 2$ |
| 2 | TOT | 22 | 70° | 42 | 390 ml |
| 3 | 18:30 | 23 | $85 \times \frac{1}{5}$ | 43 | $\frac{3}{8}$ |
| 4 | 12 | 24 | E | 44 | £747.50 |
| 5 | 30 m | 25 | E | 45 | 122° Fahrenheit |
| 6 | 20 | 26 | 9 | 46 | 1.5 m |
| 7 | 31 | 27 | E | 47 | £674 |
| 8 | C | 28 | £109.20 | 48 | £56.20 |
| 9 | 12 | 29 | 10 | 49 | $\frac{1}{2}$ of 220 |
| 10 | 12 | 30 | 3.49% | 50 | 10 cm$^2$ |
| 11 | 60° | 31 | 7 | | |
| 12 | $\frac{1}{6}$ | 32 | 1 | | |
| 13 | Q | 33 | 3 | | |
| 14 | 21 | 34 | 9 | | |
| 15 | 4 | 35 | 960 g | | |
| 16 | 6.42 | 36 | 18 cm$^2$ | | |
| 17 | $\frac{3}{5}$ | 37 | E | | |
| 18 | (5 , 2) and (2 , 5) | 38 | 0.4 of 100 | | |
| 19 | 4 | 39 | 75° | | |
| 20 | B | 40 | KN and NV | | |

# Answer Key

## Practice Paper 5

| Question | Answer | Question | Answer | Question | Answer |
|---|---|---|---|---|---|
| 1 | D | 21 | 49 700 | 41 | 160 cm |
| 2 | £9 092 045 | 22 | D | 42 | (7 , 1) |
| 3 | −18 °C | 23 | 4 | 43 | E |
| 4 | 21 | 24 | C | 44 | C |
| 5 | 3 | 25 | 422 | 45 | £102 |
| 6 | $\frac{1}{3}$ | 26 | rectangle | 46 | (6 , 6) |
| 7 | 5 | 27 | 144 g | 47 | 1000 |
| 8 | 840 | 28 | Cal | 48 | e = h |
| 9 | D | 29 | 55 | 49 | 4 |
| 10 | 0630 | 30 | 150 m | 50 | £18 |
| 11 | £15.92 | 31 | 47.65 | | |
| 12 | D | 32 | 1600 g | | |
| 13 | 0.89 | 33 | 14 202 | | |
| 14 | E | 34 | 20 | | |
| 15 | $\frac{2}{5}$ | 35 | 36p | | |
| 16 | Lisa | 36 | 10p and 20p | | |
| 17 | E | 37 | 80 | | |
| 18 | B and C | 38 | a right-angled triangle | | |
| 19 | $4\frac{1}{5} < 4.5$ | 39 | B | | |
| 20 | 8 | 40 | £200 | | |

# Answer Key

## Practice Paper 6

| Question | Answer | | Question | Answer | | Question | Answer |
|---|---|---|---|---|---|---|---|
| 1 | 4 | | 21 | B | | 41 | 48 |
| 2 | ¼ | | 22 | $2a + 2b$ | | 42 | 3.01 and 2.99 |
| 3 | B | | 23 | 2 | | 43 | 8 |
| 4 | 35 | | 24 | 45 | | 44 | 170 000 |
| 5 | B | | 25 | A | | 45 | 56 m |
| 6 | 18.33 | | 26 | 30p | | 46 | (11 , 9) |
| 7 | 70° | | 27 | over 60 | | 47 | 40% |
| 8 | C | | 28 | 4 | | 48 | Ella |
| 9 | D | | 29 | 16 | | 49 | 150° |
| 10 | 1440 | | 30 | −3 | | 50 | £9 |
| 11 | (20 , 10) | | 31 | 24 | | | |
| 12 | 25% | | 32 | 20.8 | | | |
| 13 | E | | 33 | 2014 | | | |
| 14 | 2 | | 34 | £22.50 | | | |
| 15 | D | | 35 | 4 km | | | |
| 16 | 32.2 kg | | 36 | Friday | | | |
| 17 | square centimetres | | 37 | Thursday | | | |
| | | | 38 | 26 | | | |
| 18 | 8 | | 39 | 10 | | | |
| 19 | A | | 40 | 5 | | | |
| 20 | C | | | | | | |

# Answer Sheets

# Maths
## Practice Papers 4–6

This booklet contains the answer sheets needed for Maths Practice Papers 4–6.

Please make sure you use the correct answer sheet for the test being taken, following the title at the top of each page.

The following answer sheets are included:

Maths Practice Paper 4
Maths Practice Paper 5
Maths Practice Paper 6

Published by GL Assessment, 1st Floor, Vantage London, Great West Road,
Brentford TW8 9AG.

Printed in China.

Code 6802 030
1(11.18) PF

# MATHS PRACTICE PAPER 4

| Pupil's Name | DATE OF TEST |
|---|---|
| School Name | Day  Month  Year |

| UNIQUE PUPIL NUMBER | SCHOOL NUMBER | DATE OF BIRTH |
|---|---|---|
| | | Day  Month  Year |

Please mark boxes with a thin horizontal line like this ▬.

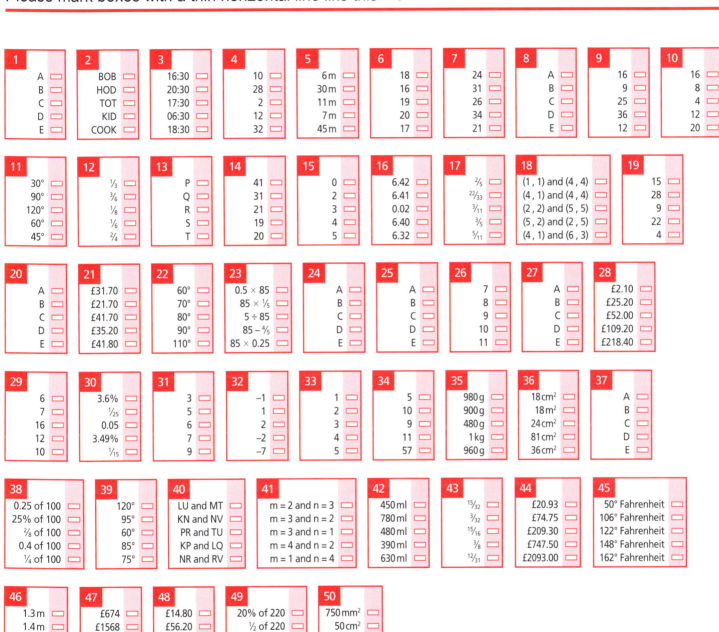

**1**
- A ▢
- B ▢
- C ▢
- D ▢
- E ▢

**2**
- BOB ▢
- HOD ▢
- TOT ▢
- KID ▢
- COOK ▢

**3**
- 16:30 ▢
- 20:30 ▢
- 17:30 ▢
- 06:30 ▢
- 18:30 ▢

**4**
- 10 ▢
- 28 ▢
- 2 ▢
- 12 ▢
- 32 ▢

**5**
- 6m ▢
- 30m ▢
- 11m ▢
- 7m ▢
- 45m ▢

**6**
- 18 ▢
- 16 ▢
- 19 ▢
- 20 ▢
- 17 ▢

**7**
- 24 ▢
- 31 ▢
- 26 ▢
- 34 ▢
- 21 ▢

**8**
- A ▢
- B ▢
- C ▢
- D ▢
- E ▢

**9**
- 16 ▢
- 9 ▢
- 25 ▢
- 36 ▢
- 12 ▢

**10**
- 16 ▢
- 8 ▢
- 4 ▢
- 12 ▢
- 20 ▢

**11**
- 30° ▢
- 90° ▢
- 120° ▢
- 60° ▢
- 45° ▢

**12**
- $\frac{1}{3}$ ▢
- $\frac{3}{6}$ ▢
- $\frac{1}{8}$ ▢
- $\frac{1}{6}$ ▢
- $\frac{2}{4}$ ▢

**13**
- P ▢
- Q ▢
- R ▢
- S ▢
- T ▢

**14**
- 41 ▢
- 31 ▢
- 21 ▢
- 19 ▢
- 20 ▢

**15**
- 0 ▢
- 2 ▢
- 3 ▢
- 4 ▢
- 5 ▢

**16**
- 6.42 ▢
- 6.41 ▢
- 0.02 ▢
- 6.40 ▢
- 6.32 ▢

**17**
- $\frac{2}{5}$ ▢
- $\frac{22}{33}$ ▢
- $\frac{3}{11}$ ▢
- $\frac{3}{5}$ ▢
- $\frac{5}{11}$ ▢

**18**
- (1, 1) and (4, 4) ▢
- (4, 1) and (4, 4) ▢
- (2, 2) and (5, 5) ▢
- (5, 2) and (2, 5) ▢
- (4, 1) and (6, 3) ▢

**19**
- 15 ▢
- 28 ▢
- 9 ▢
- 22 ▢
- 4 ▢

**20**
- A ▢
- B ▢
- C ▢
- D ▢
- E ▢

**21**
- £31.70 ▢
- £21.70 ▢
- £41.70 ▢
- £35.20 ▢
- £41.80 ▢

**22**
- 60° ▢
- 70° ▢
- 80° ▢
- 90° ▢
- 110° ▢

**23**
- 0.5 × 85 ▢
- 85 × $\frac{1}{5}$ ▢
- 5 ÷ 85 ▢
- 85 − $\frac{4}{5}$ ▢
- 85 × 0.25 ▢

**24**
- A ▢
- B ▢
- C ▢
- D ▢
- E ▢

**25**
- A ▢
- B ▢
- C ▢
- D ▢
- E ▢

**26**
- 7 ▢
- 8 ▢
- 9 ▢
- 10 ▢
- 11 ▢

**27**
- A ▢
- B ▢
- C ▢
- D ▢
- E ▢

**28**
- £2.10 ▢
- £25.20 ▢
- £52.00 ▢
- £109.20 ▢
- £218.40 ▢

**29**
- 6 ▢
- 7 ▢
- 16 ▢
- 12 ▢
- 10 ▢

**30**
- 3.6% ▢
- $\frac{1}{25}$ ▢
- 0.05 ▢
- 3.49% ▢
- $\frac{1}{15}$ ▢

**31**
- 3 ▢
- 5 ▢
- 6 ▢
- 7 ▢
- 9 ▢

**32**
- −1 ▢
- 1 ▢
- 2 ▢
- −2 ▢
- −7 ▢

**33**
- 1 ▢
- 2 ▢
- 3 ▢
- 4 ▢
- 5 ▢

**34**
- 5 ▢
- 10 ▢
- 9 ▢
- 11 ▢
- 57 ▢

**35**
- 980g ▢
- 900g ▢
- 480g ▢
- 1kg ▢
- 960g ▢

**36**
- 18cm² ▢
- 18m² ▢
- 24cm² ▢
- 81cm² ▢
- 36cm² ▢

**37**
- A ▢
- B ▢
- C ▢
- D ▢
- E ▢

**38**
- 0.25 of 100 ▢
- 25% of 100 ▢
- $\frac{2}{8}$ of 100 ▢
- 0.4 of 100 ▢
- $\frac{1}{4}$ of 100 ▢

**39**
- 120° ▢
- 95° ▢
- 60° ▢
- 85° ▢
- 75° ▢

**40**
- LU and MT ▢
- KN and NV ▢
- PR and TU ▢
- KP and LQ ▢
- NR and RV ▢

**41**
- m = 2 and n = 3 ▢
- m = 3 and n = 2 ▢
- m = 3 and n = 1 ▢
- m = 4 and n = 2 ▢
- m = 1 and n = 4 ▢

**42**
- 450ml ▢
- 780ml ▢
- 480ml ▢
- 390ml ▢
- 630ml ▢

**43**
- $\frac{15}{32}$ ▢
- $\frac{3}{32}$ ▢
- $\frac{15}{16}$ ▢
- $\frac{3}{8}$ ▢
- $\frac{12}{31}$ ▢

**44**
- £20.93 ▢
- £74.75 ▢
- £209.30 ▢
- £747.50 ▢
- £2093.00 ▢

**45**
- 50° Fahrenheit ▢
- 106° Fahrenheit ▢
- 122° Fahrenheit ▢
- 148° Fahrenheit ▢
- 162° Fahrenheit ▢

**46**
- 1.3m ▢
- 1.4m ▢
- 1.5m ▢
- 1.6m ▢
- 1.7m ▢

**47**
- £674 ▢
- £1568 ▢
- £894 ▢
- £1274 ▢
- £294 ▢

**48**
- £14.80 ▢
- £56.20 ▢
- £27.20 ▢
- £49.20 ▢
- £51.80 ▢

**49**
- 20% of 220 ▢
- $\frac{1}{2}$ of 220 ▢
- $\frac{2}{10}$ of 220 ▢
- 102 ▢
- 0.2 of 220 ▢

**50**
- 750mm² ▢
- 50cm² ▢
- 10cm² ▢
- 250cm² ▢
- 75cm² ▢

## END OF TEST

# MATHS PRACTICE PAPER 5

Pupil's Name

School Name

| DATE OF TEST | | |
|---|---|---|
| Day | Month | Year |

UNIQUE PUPIL NUMBER

SCHOOL NUMBER

| DATE OF BIRTH | | |
|---|---|---|
| Day | Month | Year |

Please mark boxes with a thin horizontal line like this ▬.

**1**
A ▭
B ▭
C ▭
D ▭
E ▭

**2**
£9 920 450 ▭
£9 092 045 ▭
£9 009 245 ▭
£9 092 450 ▭
£9 920 045 ▭

**3**
−19 °C ▭
−22 °C ▭
−14 °C ▭
−21 °C ▭
−18 °C ▭

**4**
13 ▭
17 ▭
19 ▭
21 ▭
23 ▭

**5**
1 ▭
2 ▭
3 ▭
4 ▭
5 ▭

**6**
½ ▭
¾ ▭
¼ ▭
⅓ ▭
⅔ ▭

**7**
6 ▭
7 ▭
4 ▭
5 ▭
8 ▭

**8**
84 ▭
336 ▭
840 ▭
420 ▭
168 ▭

**9**
A ▭
B ▭
C ▭
D ▭
E ▭

**10**
0527 ▭
0630 ▭
0645 ▭
0700 ▭
0712 ▭

**11**
£15.92 ▭
£15.98 ▭
£16.00 ▭
£16.02 ▭
£16.08 ▭

**12**
A ▭
B ▭
C ▭
D ▭
E ▭

**13**
0.99 ▭
0.09 ▭
0.91 ▭
0.19 ▭
0.89 ▭

**14**
A ▭
B ▭
C ▭
D ▭
E ▭

**15**
⅕ ▭
½ ▭
⅖ ▭
⁶⁄₁₀ ▭
⁶⁄₁₃ ▭

**16**
Kieran ▭
Haq ▭
Harriet ▭
Lisa ▭
Jake ▭

**17**
A ▭
B ▭
C ▭
D ▭
E ▭

**18**
A and B ▭
B and C ▭
C and D ▭
A and C ▭
B and D ▭

**19**
$4\frac{1}{5} < 4.5$ ▭
$4\frac{1}{2} < 4.5$ ▭
$4\frac{1}{5} > 4.5$ ▭
$4\frac{1}{2} > 4.5$ ▭
$4\frac{1}{5} = 4.5$ ▭

**20**
0 ▭
4 ▭
6 ▭
8 ▭
10 ▭

**21**
9443 ▭
44 730 ▭
49 700 ▭
54 670 ▭
9 170 644 ▭

**22**
A ▭
B ▭
C ▭
D ▭
E ▭

**23**
4 ▭
2 ▭
1 ▭
3 ▭
5 ▭

**24**
A ▭
B ▭
C ▭
D ▭
E ▭

**25**
380 ▭
436 ▭
408 ▭
394 ▭
422 ▭

**26**
square ▭
rectangle ▭
rhombus ▭
quadrilateral ▭
trapezium ▭

**27**
1.44 g ▭
0.144 g ▭
144 g ▭
86.9 g ▭
1.44 kg ▭

**28**
Annie ▭
Ben ▭
Cal ▭
Donna ▭
Esther ▭

**29**
55 ▭
35 ▭
25 ▭
45 ▭
65 ▭

**30**
75 m ▭
150 m ▭
240 m ▭
300 m ▭
330 m ▭

**31**
44.5 ▭
47.05 ▭
47.5 ▭
47.65 ▭
53.5 ▭

**32**
800 g ▭
1050 g ▭
1250 g ▭
1500 g ▭
1600 g ▭

**33**
7101 ▭
14 202 ▭
14 204 ▭
14 991 ▭
15 774 ▭

**34**
20 ▭
16 ▭
19 ▭
15 ▭
21 ▭

**35**
36p ▭
24p ▭
12p ▭
48p ▭
18p ▭

**36**
1p and 2p ▭
2p and 5p ▭
5p and 10p ▭
10p and 20p ▭
20p and £1 ▭

**37**
20 ▭
80 ▭
64 ▭
100 ▭
40 ▭

**38**
a right-angled triangle ▭
an equilateral triangle ▭
a square ▭
a rectangle ▭
a parallelogram ▭

**39**
A ▭
B ▭
C ▭
D ▭
E ▭

**40**
£128 ▭
£180 ▭
£200 ▭
£192 ▭
£188 ▭

**41**
480 cm ▭
1.6 m ▭
250 cm ▭
320 cm ▭
160 cm ▭

**42**
(7 , 1) ▭
(7 , 2) ▭
(5 , 1) ▭
(2 , 7) ▭
(7 , 3) ▭

**43**
A ▭
B ▭
C ▭
D ▭
E ▭

**44**
A ▭
B ▭
C ▭
D ▭
E ▭

**45**
£51 ▭
£102 ▭
£5.10 ▭
£127.50 ▭
£25.50 ▭

**46**
(4 , 4) ▭
(6 , 6) ▭
(6 , 8) ▭
(8 , 8) ▭
(4 , 6) ▭

**47**
1000 ▭
100 ▭
10 000 ▭
100 000 ▭
10 ▭

**48**
a = b ▭
d = h ▭
a = c + d ▭
e = h ▭
f = g ▭

**49**
2 ▭
6 ▭
4 ▭
8 ▭
1 ▭

**50**
£12 ▭
£13.50 ▭
£15 ▭
£16.20 ▭
£18 ▭

Pupil's Name

School Name

UNIQUE PUPIL NUMBER

SCHOOL NUMBER

DATE OF TEST
| Day | Month | Year |

DATE OF BIRTH
| Day | Month | Year |

Please mark boxes with a thin horizontal line like this ▬.

**1**
- 4
- 1
- 8
- 6
- 2

**2**
- ½
- ⅓
- ¼
- ⅕
- ⅙

**3**
- A
- B
- C
- D
- E

**4**
- 31
- 32
- 33
- 34
- 35

**5**
- A
- B
- C
- D
- E

**6**
- 14.28
- 18.33
- 18.3
- 18.88
- 17.33

**7**
- 10°
- 30°
- 50°
- 70°
- 90°

**8**
- A
- B
- C
- D
- E

**9**
- A
- B
- C
- D
- E

**10**
- 1008
- 3024
- 1152
- 1011
- 1440

**11**
- (10 , 5)
- (5 , 10)
- (20 , 10)
- (10 , 20)
- (15 , 10)

**12**
- 10%
- 15%
- 20%
- 25%
- 30%

**13**
- A
- B
- C
- D
- E

**14**
- 2
- 4
- 6
- 8
- 10

**15**
- A
- B
- C
- D
- E

**16**
- 32.2 kg
- 22.2 kg
- 31.2 kg
- 21.2 kg
- 33.2 kg

**17**
- metres
- square metres
- centimetres
- millimetres
- square centimetres

**18**
- 2
- 4
- 6
- 8
- 10

**19**
- A
- B
- C
- D
- E

**20**
- A
- B
- C
- D
- E

**21**
- A
- B
- C
- D
- E

**22**
- $a + b$
- $2a + 2b$
- $a \times b$
- $a \times 2b$
- $2a \times 2b$

**23**
- 2
- 3
- 4
- 5
- 6

**24**
- 25
- 35
- 45
- 55
- 65

**25**
- A
- B
- C
- D
- E

**26**
- 60p
- 20p
- 40p
- 50p
- 30p

**27**
- 0 to 20
- 21 to 40
- 40 and under
- over 60
- 61 to 80

**28**
- 3
- 4
- 5
- 6
- 7

**29**
- 36
- 14
- 16
- 25
- 12

**30**
- 0
- −4
- −2
- −1
- −3

**31**
- 24
- 20
- 4
- 22
- 28

**32**
- 0.28
- 2.08
- 20.8
- 28
- 208

**33**
- 2013
- 2014
- 2015
- 2016
- 2017

**34**
- £24.00
- £21.50
- £22.00
- £20.00
- £22.50

**35**
- 2 km
- 4 km
- 6 km
- 8 km
- 10 km

**36**
- Friday
- Saturday
- Thursday
- Sunday
- Monday

**37**
- Monday
- Tuesday
- Wednesday
- Thursday
- Friday

**38**
- 13
- 16 ¼
- 26
- 52
- 130

**39**
- 8
- 9
- 10
- 11
- 12

**40**
- 1
- 2
- 3
- 4
- 5

**41**
- 48
- 12
- 24
- 6
- 96

**42**
- 3.01 and 2.91
- 3.01 and 2.99
- 3.11 and 2.91
- 3.11 and 2.99
- 3.19 and 2.91

**43**
- 9
- 11
- 16
- 8
- 10

**44**
- 45 000
- 30 000
- 200 000
- 55 000
- 170 000

**45**
- 40 m
- 42 m
- 48 m
- 52 m
- 56 m

**46**
- (9 , 11)
- (10 , 12)
- (10 , 9)
- (11 , 9)
- (11 , 15)

**47**
- 25%
- 30%
- 33%
- 40%
- 50%

**48**
- Adi
- Bethan
- Carlos
- Danny
- Ella

**49**
- 110°
- 150°
- 120°
- 210°
- 30°

**50**
- £4
- £5
- £7
- £8
- £9

# END OF TEST

ISBN 978-0-70872-759-1